GUEVARA

Che

Che

Kate Havelin

Twenty-First Century Books
Minneapolis

To those who work to make their country and world a better place through peaceful means. The ballot box is more potent than bullets.

Twenty-First Century Books
A division of Lerner Publishing Group
241 First Avenue North
Minneapolis, MN 55401 U.S.A.

Website addresses: www.lernerbooks.com
www.biography.com

Library of Congress Cataloging-in-Publication Data

Havelin, Kate, 1961–
    Che Guevara / by Kate Havelin.
      p.   cm. — (Biography)
    Includes bibliographical references and index.
    ISBN-13: 978–0–8225–5951–1 (lib. bdg. : alk. paper)
    ISBN-10: 0–8225–5951–X (lib. bdg. : alk. paper)
      1. Guevara, Ernesto, 1928–1967. 2. Cuba—History—1959–
    3. Guerrillas—Latin America—Biography. I. Title. II. Biography
    (Twenty-First Century Books (Firm))
    F2849.22.G85H38 2007
    980.03'5092—dc22   2005034948

Manufactured in the United States of America
1 2 3 4 5 6 – BP – 12 11 10 09 08 07

CONTENTS

In Cuba in the late 1950s, Che Guevara (center) *discusses an upcoming battle with his fellow rebels.*

Chapter **ONE**

YOUNG ERNESTO

CHE GUEVARA AND HIS FELLOW REBELS WERE UNDER attack. The determined band of eighty-two men had just landed in Cuba with their leader, Fidel Castro. Their mission: to overthrow Cuban dictator Fulgencio Batista. But Batista's soldiers were ready for the rebels.

The army pounced on the weary and confused revolutionaries. Che and the others had to flee to save their lives. Che was the doctor for the rebels. When the Cuban soldiers attacked, he had to make a split-second decision—should he save a first-aid kit or a box of ammunition?

Che Guevara, a medical doctor who dreamed of being a revolutionary, chose the bullets. He grabbed the box and began running, trying to escape the soldiers' bullets. Within minutes, a bullet hit Che in the neck. He thought he was dying. He slumped to the ground.

He remembered a Jack London short story, "To Build a Fire." It was about a man who freezes to death in the frigid Yukon region of Alaska and Canada. Like that character, Che felt peaceful, ready for death. But another rebel grabbed him and helped him run away from the soldiers. The bullet had just grazed Che's neck, so the injury did not turn out to be serious.

Guevara, Castro, and a few other rebels escaped the soldiers and hid in the Sierra Maestra Mountains of southern Cuba. Less than two dozen of the eighty-two rebels reached the safety of the mountains. Government soldiers killed the rebels they captured.

During the next two years, Che Guevara, Fidel Castro, and other revolutionaries fought against Batista's army. In the end, the rebels won. Fidel Castro became Cuba's leader, and he made Che Guevara the second most powerful person in the country. It was an amazing achievement for a middle-class Argentinean. Che had never even visited Cuba before landing on the shore with Castro and his fellow rebels.

A Boy with Asthma

Ernesto Guevara de la Serna was born on June 14, 1928, in Rosario, a remote jungle region of Argentina. His parents, Celia de la Serna and Ernesto Guevara

Fidel Castro (seated) *set up the rebels' base camp deep in Cuba's Sierra Maestra Mountains.*

Lynch, were from Buenos Aires, the cosmopolitan capital of Argentina. Both Celia and Ernesto came from upper-class families whose ancestors included Spanish nobles. Celia's father had been a congressman and ambassador, but both of her parents had died when she was young. Ernesto Guevara Lynch's Spanish-Irish family had once been quite wealthy, but by the time he was born, the fortune was gone.

Ernesto owned a boatbuilding company with his cousin in a suburb of Buenos Aires. When Ernesto and Celia married, the couple used the bride's inheritance money to buy 500 acres (200 hectares) of land far from Buenos Aires. They planned to farm yerba maté, a plant used to make a popular South American tea drink. Celia and Ernesto likely left Buenos Aires to hide the fact that Celia was pregnant before their marriage.

Ernesto was still a toddler when his family moved back to Buenos Aires. In December 1929, Ernesto's first sibling, a girl named Celia, was born. By the age of three, Ernesto had developed asthma, a lung condition that causes wheezing and trouble breathing. Asthma attacks may be triggered by many things, including dust, pollen, animal dander (small flakes of skin or hair), and a variety of common foods. Ernesto's parents kept a detailed diary of everything he ate and everything he did so they could try to prevent his asthma attacks.

In 1932, when Ernesto was four, his family—including a new baby brother, Roberto—moved to Alta Gracia, in Argentina's central highlands. Ernesto's parents hoped that the drier climate would ease their son's breathing problems. The Guevaras stayed in Alta Gracia for the next eleven years. During that time,

Ernesto and Celia had two more children: Ana Mariá, born in 1934, and Juan Martín, born in 1943.

Ernesto, whose family called him Tete, spent his childhood playing with his brothers and sisters and the neighbor children. He bicycled, swam, and pretended to be cops and robbers or soldiers. But because of his asthma, Ernesto didn't attend school until he was nine years old. Before that, his mother Celia taught Ernesto at home.

Ernesto's father never managed to find steady work in Alta Gracia. For a time, he had a landscaping job at the local golf course. Mostly the family relied on Celia's small inheritance and income from the family's yerba maté farm. Neither Celia nor Ernesto was good at budgeting their money. Sometimes they didn't have enough money to pay their rent. They had to move often, but they spent several years in a comfortable home called Villa Nydia. It had three bedrooms as well as servants' quarters.

Ernesto was sometimes sick for days, staying in bed struggling to breathe. He read for hours, savoring adventure stories written by Jack London and Jules Verne. He played chess with his father. When he was sick, Ernesto ate little. When he recovered, he gobbled lots of food. Celia and Ernesto believed that swimming helped their son, so the family joined a swim club. Ernesto also played soccer, golf, and table tennis. He liked to hike, practice target shooting, and have rock fights. Ernesto's father worried that the sports were too much for his son's weak lungs. Sometimes Ernesto coughed and wheezed and had to be carried home from wherever he was playing.

Ernesto was more interested in sports than school. His grades were average or below average. He was known for daredevil pranks such as drinking ink, eating chalk, and exploring an abandoned mine shaft. After Ernesto's first year of high school, his family moved to the city of Córdoba, where they lived for four years.

NICKNAMES

Although Ernesto was thin and smaller than other boys his age, he was determined. When he tried out for the local rugby team in high school, Ernesto proved he could be fearless. Alberto Granado, the older brother of one of Ernesto's friends, was coaching the team. Granado remembered seeing Ernesto run down the field, charging the player with the ball, yelling, "Look out, here comes Furious Serna!" His friends nicknamed him Fuser, a shortened version of his call, "Furious Serna."

Fuser was one of several nicknames Ernesto picked up when he was young. His friends starting calling him El Palao, or "Baldy," after he got a crew cut. Because he dressed sloppily and sometimes wore mismatched shoes, Ernesto was nicknamed Chancho, meaning "the pig." People also called him El Loco (Crazy) Guevara because of his daredevil stunts.

Córdoba, Argentina, was an old Spanish colonial city when Che went to high school there. Jesuits (Roman Catholic priests) founded Córdoba University (above) there in 1613.

Despite his reckless behavior at times, Ernesto did show some concern for his own safety. In 1943 Argentinean generals overthrew the country's president, Ramón Castillo. The generals postponed elections. They tried to keep people from protesting by closing down all political parties and firing university professors who spoke out against the harsh policies. Many students and teachers protested. Alberto Granado and other student protesters were arrested and put in jail.

Ernesto and his friends visited Alberto in jail. Alberto asked Ernesto and other high school students to hold a protest march to pressure the government to free the jailed students. Ernesto, who was fifteen, refused. He said he would not march against the police unless he had a gun to protect himself. Several months later, Alberto and the other students were freed from jail. Even though Ernesto had not joined the march, he and Alberto remained friends.

By the time Ernesto was sixteen, he finally began growing taller. He was a good-looking young man, with dark hair and eyes. He had pale, clear skin and a smile that showed his confidence. As he grew older, Ernesto continued to read many books. He loved novels and poetry. Sometimes he locked himself in the bathroom for hours so he could read quietly.

After graduating from high school in 1945, Ernesto continued to study. He read the entire twenty-five-volume *Contemporary History of the Modern World*. He wrote 165 pages detailing what he thought about life, love, death, and religion. His notebooks also included brief biographies of the thinkers and philosophers whose works he had read. Ernesto thought about becoming an engineer. But when his paternal grandmother died, he decided to study medicine instead. He had been close to his grandmother. When she was dying, he quit his job and spent the last seventeen days of her life with her. Her death left Ernesto very sad. He dreamed of becoming a famous

medical researcher who would find cures for dis-
eases, including asthma. He enrolled at the University
of Buenos Aires and also worked at an asthma clinic
with a leading researcher, Dr. Salvador Pisani.

Buenos Aires
(right) *was a*
modern city when
Ernesto went to
college there in
the 1940s.

THE REWARDS OF TRAVEL

After his third year of medical school, twenty-two-year-old Ernesto planned an ambitious trip by himself. Instead of hitchhiking, he rode a bicycle equipped with a small motor. He set out on January 1, 1950, to explore the hilly Córdoba Province and visit his friend Alberto Granado, who was working in northern Argentina.

This trip marked the first time Ernesto kept a travel diary. He wrote about the landscape as well as the hospitals and jails where he was able to spend the night for free. "The spirit [of a place] is reflected in the patients of its hospitals, the inmates at the police station and the anxious pedestrian one chats to while the Rio Grande displays its turbulent, swollen waters below," he wrote.

Ernesto wanted to get to know his country while challenging himself. On his second night of biking, he reached a town at 11:00 P.M. "My body was screaming for a mattress, but my will won out and I continued," he wrote in his diary. He kept going, and at two in the morning, when it started to rain, he recalled, "I laughed at the downpour."

Ernesto wasn't pedaling the entire time. Sometimes he attached his bike to the back of a truck or car and was pulled along for miles. Still, the journey took a toll on both rider and bicycle. He covered more than 2,480 miles (3,991 kilometers). When Ernesto returned to Buenos Aires, he brought his bike in for repairs. The company that made the bicycle learned about Ernesto's ambitious journey and asked if he would be in an advertisement. Ernesto agreed, and the company fixed his bike for free.

In his first year at the university, Ernesto was called up to serve in the military. But army doctors decided that he wasn't fit enough to be a soldier because of his lung problems.

Although his asthma kept him from serving in the army, it didn't stop Ernesto from traveling. When he wasn't studying, Ernesto liked to leave Buenos Aires and hitchhike around Argentina. His travels made him want to see more of his country and the rest of South America.

Seated on his bicycle, Guevara poses for a photo in Córdoba, Argentina, in 1950.

Chapter **TWO**

TRAVELING WITH MIAL

AFTER HIS FIFTH YEAR OF MEDICAL SCHOOL, WHEN Guevara was close to graduating, he once again hit the road. This time he traveled with Alberto Granado. The two told friends and family that they planned to go west to Chile, but their true goal was much grander. They wanted to explore the length of South America, from Argentina to Venezuela. From there they hoped to fly to the United States.

Granado called Guevara Fuser, his old rugby nickname. Guevara referred to his friend as Mial, short for Mi Alberto (My Alberto). They left Buenos Aires on January 4, 1952, riding Granado's vintage motorcycle. The bike also had a nickname: *Poderosa II*, or "the Mighty One." Their first stop was Miramar, where they visited Mariá del Carmen Ferreyra. Chichina, as she was known, was an heiress. Guevara had fallen in love with her at a wedding a year earlier. Guevara and Granado planned to spend two days in Miramar, but their visit stretched to eight days.

After leaving Miramar, Guevara got sick. He was hospitalized for several days with a high fever. When he recovered, he and Granado again took to the road. Guevara got a letter from Chichina—she didn't intend to wait for him to return. He was brokenhearted. "I read and reread the incredible letter," he recalled. "Just like that, all [my] dreams . . . came crashing down."

FEARING FOR HIS LIFE

Loaded with backpacks, a tent, food, and two men, the Mighty One strained to steer straight. Guevara noted, "The motorbike is very hard to control, with extra weight on a rack behind the center of gravity tending to lift the front wheel, and the slightest lapse in concentration sends us flying." In one day, their motorcycle crashed nine times as it wobbled over gravel and sand roads. Granado kept a supply of wire to repair the motorcycle.

The two men didn't have enough money to buy everything they needed, so they had to rough it. The villages they traveled through didn't have motels. Sometimes Guevara and Granado camped in their tent. But they liked having a roof over their heads at night when it was cold. They often asked to spend the night in local jails or hospitals or villagers' houses, garages, or barns.

One night shortly before they reached Chile, the travelers slept in a shed. Guevara was nervous. The caretaker of the property had warned them about a puma that was prowling the area. Guevara slept with the pistol his father had given him for the trip. Early the next morning, an animal scratched at the door. Guevara saw the animal's eyes over the half-open door. He reached for his gun and shot. "It was pure instinct; the brakes of intelligence failed," he wrote later. He heard the caretaker and his wife scream. Instead of shooting a puma, Guevara had killed Bobby, a dog belonging to the caretaker's wife.

After a month of traveling, Guevara and Granado crossed the border into Chile. They enjoyed the hospitality of the Chilean people. Small newspapers interviewed the pair, who claimed to be specialists in leprosy, a contagious disease that left people disfigured. Granado was a chemist who had studied leprosy, but Guevara was not yet a full-fledged medical doctor. Still, the headline in one village newspaper read, "Two Argentine Leprosy Experts Tour Latin America by Motorcycle."

As they made their way through Chile, Guevara and Granado talked about renaming their motorcycle *Weakling II*. Flat tires, worn parts, and faulty steering made riding a challenge. Two months after the men had left home, the motorcycle's gearbox and steering column cracked. The bike was doomed. The men wrapped it in their tent to protect its worn frame. Granado wrote, "I felt as though we were placing a shroud on the dead body of a loyal friend. . . . I gave the bike a gentle pat and walked away, sad and upset."

The two friends began hitchhiking. Then they hid aboard a small ship, the *San Antonio,* which was docked in Valparaíso, Chile. The stowaways were quickly discovered hiding in the ship's smelly toilet. The captain made Guevara clean out the toilets. Granado got off easier, peeling vegetables. At night the

In the 1950s, Valparaíso, Chile, had a busy seaport.

men played cards with the captain. They saw flying fish, tropical fish with winglike fins that seem to glide through the air. Guevara and Granado stayed on board until the *San Antonio* reached Antofagasta, Chile, where they continued heading north by foot.

LIFE STORIES ALONG THE ROAD

Without a motorcycle to speed their journey, the hitchhikers spent more time talking with people along the way. They played soccer with men building rural roads and later lost a farting contest to the road builders. They rode along with two young truckers who liked to sing tangos—and almost died when the truck's axle broke and the truck nearly careened off a cliff. Guevara fulfilled a lifelong dream to swim across the wide Amazon River.

The men tagged along with hunters in search of monkeys and later ate roasted monkey meat. Granado remarked that it looked like "a newborn baby." Other times they went days without food and learned to scrounge to get by. "Waking up in this sleeping bag, half-buried in the sweet-smelling grass I thought to myself that this is what I had always wanted," Granado wrote. "A journey like this, with no other concern than to see and get to know our America by my own means."

Guevara and Granado met many people whose stories moved them. They talked with peasants who worked long hours doing dangerous jobs for little money. They met poor people who generously shared their scant food and shelter. In return, Guevara and Granado shared their medical expertise. Guevara went to see an old woman with asthma and heart problems. He knew there was little he could do to help the dying woman, but he gave her his motion sickness pills to ease her discomfort. "It is at times like this, when a doctor is conscious of his complete powerlessness, that he longs for change," Guevara wrote in his diary. "It's time that those who govern spend less time publicizing their own virtues and more money, much more money, funding socially useful works."

Later Guevara and Granado trekked through a desolate desert on their way to visit Chuquicamata, a massive copper mine in Chile. In the bitter desert night, they shared bread and yerba maté with a starving couple. The husband had been fired from his job and sent to prison for three months because he belonged to the Communist Party. Communists believe that the government, rather than individuals, should own all property. Each person should work and be paid according to his or her skills and needs. But Chile's leaders opposed Communism and punished citizens who supported it.

The couple Guevara and Granado met had been forced to leave their children with a neighbor and take to the road to find work. "They had not one single miserable blanket to cover themselves with, so we gave them one of ours and Alberto and I wrapped the other

While Guevara and Granado were in Chile in 1952, Carlos Ibáñez del Campo was the nation's president.

around us as best we could," Guevara wrote. "It was one of the coldest times in my life, but also one which made me feel a little more brotherly toward this, strange, for me at least, human species."

Guevara and Granado met many people who suffered because they didn't have food, medicine, education, or safe working conditions. Seeing so many poor people made Guevara think that society needed to change. He began to think more about how governments should help people.

Visiting Lepers

From Chile, Guevara and Granado made their way to Peru. While traveling, Guevara sometimes had asthma attacks. When needed, Granado gave his friend emergency shots of adrenaline, medicine that helped him breathe. The men stayed in one place until Guevara was well enough to travel again. But the travelers met people whose health problems were far worse when they visited leprosariums, hospitals for people with leprosy.

LEPROSY

Leprosy is mentioned in the Bible and is thought to have existed as far back as 1000 B.C. Leprosy, also called Hansen's disease, is still common in tropical and subtropical countries. The disease is caused by a type of bacteria, and most doctors believe it spreads through coughing or sneezing. Leprosy tends to occur in crowded, unsanitary places. But people in developed countries such as the United States can also get Hansen's disease.

The long-term disease can cause nerve damage and deformity. But treatment with antibiotic drugs can help people with leprosy live a normal life.

Guevara and Granado weren't afraid of spending time with lepers, and the patients were grateful for the visitors. Granado helped out in the leprosarium clinics and laboratories. At the leprosy hospital in San Pablo, Peru, patients hosted a party for Guevara's twenty-fourth birthday. They contributed money for the travelers to continue their trip.

"THE MOST IMPORTANT PERSON ON THE JOURNEY"

The hitchhikers traveled to Lima, Peru, to meet Dr. Hugo Pesce, who was in charge of caring for Peru's lepers. Years earlier, Pesce had been exiled to the

Andes Mountains because he was a Communist. But he continued his research and discovered that mosquitoes transmit the disease malaria. He also found a treatment for leprosy. Granado called the doctor "the most important person we have met on the journey so far."

The hitchhikers spent three weeks visiting Dr. Pesce. Guevara was impressed to meet a medical person who was truly dedicated to the common good. Years later Guevara wrote to Pesce that he had "without knowing it, perhaps provoked a great change in my attitude toward life and society."

Since 1550 the Cathedral of Lima, Peru, has dominated the Plaza de Armas, Lima's central public square.

Guevara nicknamed Dr. Pesce the Maestro (the Master) because of his accomplishments in medicine, politics, poetry, and philosophy. The doctor gave his visitors clothes, food, money, and books. He asked them to read a book he had written called *Latitudes*

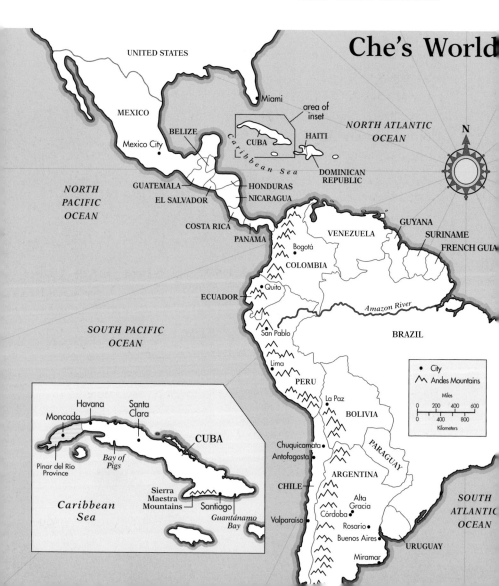

Che's World

of Silence. When it was time to say good-bye, Pesce pressed Guevara for his opinion of the book. "Look, Doctor, it's not a good book," Guevara said bluntly. "The description of the landscape says nothing new. . . . It's a pessimistic book that doesn't seem to have come from the pen of either a scientist or a Communist."

Pesce took Guevara's criticism calmly. Granado was furious with his friend for insulting the doctor's book. Granado realized, "Ernesto cannot tell a lie."

The two friends continued onward to Bogotá, Colombia, where police found and took a knife that Guevara had. When he and Granado argued with the police, both men were arrested. Police threatened to force them to leave the country. Colombia was on the verge of a revolution. Granado and Guevara followed the advice of students they met and left the country quickly.

They went to Venezuela, where Granado decided to stay and work at a leprosarium. In July 1952, seven months after their journey began, the two friends said good-bye. When they had begun their trip, the men had hoped to reach the United States. Once Granado stopped in Venezuela, Guevara continued north alone. He caught a transport plane to Miami, Florida, where he stayed with a cousin of his ex-girlfriend Chichina. After a month, he flew home to Buenos Aires to finish medical school.

Guevara and Ferrer visited the ancient Inca city of Machu Picchu in Peru. Guevara had a keen interest in archaeological sites in South America.

Chapter **THREE**

BECOMING CHE

AFTER GRADUATING FROM MEDICAL SCHOOL IN
1953, Guevara was offered a job working with his
mentor, Dr. Pisani. But the new doctor wasn't ready
to settle down. He wanted to travel again. This time,
he and a childhood friend, Carlos Ferrer, intended to
explore Bolivia and Peru, visiting Inca ruins. The
men left by train, headed for adventure.

In La Paz, Bolivia, Guevara and Ferrer saw many
people in the city carrying guns. Every day the men
heard gunshots, and sometimes they saw people
wounded or killed. A group called the National
Revolutionary Movement had taken control of
Bolivia and was dramatically changing the country.
The new leaders wanted to give Bolivians more rights

and education. Other political groups opposed the revolutionaries.

FROM BOLIVIA TO GUATEMALA AND MEXICO

From Bolivia Guevara and his friend Ferrer went their separate ways. Guevara wanted to go to Guatemala to learn more about the Central American country that was most independent of the United States. Ferrer went on to Quito, the capital of Ecuador.

The United States exerted control over many Latin American economies either directly, through ownership of large industries, or indirectly, as a key trading partner. For example, although the revolutionary government in Bolivia controlled the country's valuable mines, the United States still influenced the economy by buying most of Bolivia's exports. Leftist thinkers—those who favored radical change or reform of the established order—wanted to reduce U.S. power in Latin America.

In Guatemala Guevara met Hilda Gadea, a Peruvian activist who had been forced to leave her country. Guevara and Gadea spent hours talking politics. She soon fell in love with him. They became a couple, but Guevara was not interested in a serious relationship. He wanted to travel, not settle down with one woman.

Gadea had a job in the Guatemalan government. President Jacobo Arbenz, a leftist, was working to reform his country. New laws gave peasants control of the farms they worked and allowed people to vote in elections even if they could not read. In Guatemala Guevara was inspired to become a revolutionary himself. His time there, along with his travels through South America, shaped Guevara's political beliefs and led him to embrace Communism. He thought that this political and economic system would provide more opportunities and justice for poor people.

The U.S. government, however, strongly opposed Communism. Officials in the United States feared that Arbenz's policies would lead to Communism in Guatemala and then in other Latin American countries.

On June 17, 1954, a few days after Guevara celebrated his twenty-sixth birthday in Guatemala, President Arbenz was violently ousted from power. Four hundred Guatemalan military officers, armed and trained by the U.S. Central Intelligence Agency (CIA), invaded Guatemala from the nearby countries of Honduras and Nicaragua. Guevara wanted to join the fight to keep Arbenz in power. But the Guatemalan leader quickly stepped down on June 27. Guevara was disappointed that the revolution ended abruptly, before he got a chance to fight.

He and Hilda Gadea ended up in Mexico City, Mexico, where they lived with a friend of hers. Guevara found odd jobs working as a guard, an allergy researcher, and a photographer. He wanted to earn money so he could travel to Venezuela, to Cuba, to the United States, and then to cross the Atlantic. "I still have a fantastic urge to travel through Europe," Guevara wrote to his mother. He explained that even though he believed in revolution and the Communist Party, he hadn't committed to either yet. "I am a complete bum and I don't feel like having my career interrupted by an iron discipline," he wrote. Guevara believed that being a Communist and working to change society required a great effort—more than he was willing to give at that point.

In Mexico City, Guevara met a group of Cubans who wanted to overthrow the government of Cuba's dictator, Fulgencio Batista. Batista was considered a

Cuban dictator Fulgencio Batista led a series of corrupt governments in Cuba from the 1930s to the 1950s.

"strongman," a term for a leader who rules harshly and dominates his people. Like other Latin American strongmen, Batista came from the military. He twice overthrew elected Cuban leaders and seized power. Batista became a dictator, someone who rules with absolute power and control. Batista's government was corrupt, with close ties to American gangsters. Nevertheless, the U.S. government backed Batista, because he allowed U.S. companies to control most of Cuba's rich farmlands and mines.

The Cubans whom Guevara met had been part of an earlier rebellion against Batista on July 26, 1953. Led by a young lawyer named Fidel Castro, the rebels had overrun an army barracks at Moncada, Cuba. They were arrested soon after the attack, however. Fidel, his brother Raúl, and other Cuban rebels were sentenced to fifteen years in jail for their plot to overthrow Batista's government. In the meantime, some of Castro's supporters had made their way to Mexico City.

MEETING FIDEL

With his strong interest in politics, Guevara continued to meet and talk with the Cuban rebels. They nicknamed him Che, a common expression that Guevara and other Argentineans used. It's a word used to mean "friend" as "pal," "dude," or "man" are used in many English speaking countries. In July 1955, Fidel Castro arrived in Mexico after being pardoned by Batista and released from jail. The Cubans introduced Che to Fidel. Guevara described Castro as "an intelligent young fellow who is very sure of himself and extraordinarily bold; I think we like each other."

Castro asked the young Argentinean doctor to join his Cuban revolution. Guevara said yes immediately. He and the Cubans began training for their planned attack on Cuba. They took long hikes carrying heavy packs. They wanted to get stronger and learn to withstand tough conditions. They needed to be in good

Too Little Food, Too Few Toilets

Many Cubans were hungry for revolution—literally. In the early 1950s, large numbers of Cuban people didn't have enough food to eat. The average Cuban earned just six pesos a week, the equivalent of six dollars a week. Many Cubans didn't even earn that small amount. The country's unemployment rate was very high—one out of every four Cubans who could work didn't have a job.

Living conditions on the island were also harsh. Less than half of the country's homes had running water. Even fewer had flush toilets. More than half the people living in rural areas didn't have any kind of toilets.

Without adequate sanitation, jobs, and food, many Cubans were ready for a change. They were ready for a new government, especially one that promised to improve the quality of life in Cuba.

Fidel Castro (left) *asked Guevara* (right) *to join his Cuban revolution. Guevara was soon deeply involved in the struggle.*

shape to be successful guerrilla fighters. In guerrilla warfare, small groups of fighters use sneak attacks against more organized and usually larger numbers of regular troops. Castro believed he could win a guerrilla war against Cuba's government.

Soon after Guevara decided to join the Cuban rebels, Hilda Gadea told him that she was pregnant. On August 18, 1955, the couple married. Guevara wasn't excited. He didn't love Hilda and didn't want to be married. In his diary, he wrote, "For me, it is an uncomfortable episode . . . she gets her way—the way I see it, for a short while, although she hopes it will be lifelong." A few months after their wedding, the couple took a brief honeymoon. They traveled to Mexico's

The Mayan ruins at Chichén Itzá on Mexico's Yucatán Peninsula are famous for their stark beauty. On his honeymoon in this region, Che paid more attention to the ruins than to his new wife, Hilda.

Yucatán Peninsula to see the Mayan ruins there. Hilda was seasick on the boat trip. Che laughed. He ran up the steps to the ruins. She was tired. Her letters to friends talked about the romance of being with him. His letters described the scenery—and never once mentioned her.

In February 1956, Hilda gave birth to a baby girl, Hilda Beatriz Guevara. Che and Hilda nicknamed their daughter Hildita. "I'm very happy with her," Guevara wrote to his mother. "My communist soul is bursting with joy—she's just like [Chinese Communist leader] Mao. . . . You can already see the . . . baldness in the middle of her [head], the kindly eyes of the leader and the protuberant jowls [round cheeks]."

A few months after Hildita's birth, Guevara left Mexico City to train with about forty Cubans. They had judged one another's skills as soldiers, and the Cubans voted Guevara a leader. He became the rebels' chief of staff. His first task involved acting. He pretended to be a rich Salvadoran who wanted to buy a ranch outside the city. Guevara agreed to pay eight dollars a month rent to stay in the expensive ranch while his Salvadoran workers—who were actually the Cuban rebels—fixed it up. The men didn't want to draw attention to themselves. They wanted to prepare for their Cuban takeover without Mexicans knowing what they were doing.

ARRESTED

Despite their efforts to avoid attention, the rebels were noticed. In June 1956, Mexican police raided the ranch. They arrested Castro and about two dozen other Cubans. Castro was charged with plotting to assassinate Cuba's president. Guevara was arrested a few days later, shortly after his twenty-eighth birthday.

He told police he was in Mexico as a tourist. Later he told them more about how he was the doctor for Castro's rebel army and about why armed revolt was necessary. He was charged only with staying in Mexico longer than his visa (permit to stay in the country) allowed. He and the others were put in prison.

From jail Guevara wrote his parents a letter, noting, "My future is joined to the Cuban Revolution. Either triumph with it or die." The first known picture of Guevara and Castro together was taken in a Mexican prison cell.

Mexican police released Castro and most of the Cubans after a month. But Guevara and one other man spent almost two months in jail. Castro swore he would not leave Mexico and begin his revolution while some of his men were still locked up. Castro was angry that Guevara had told the Mexican authorities about their plans for revolt. Yet Castro paid a bribe to free Che and the other rebel. Guevara was grateful for Castro's help.

After his release, Guevara went home and spent three days with his wife and baby. From there he went into hiding with Castro's other rebels and prepared for revolution. Castro unveiled a written plan for how he would liberate, or free, Cuba. He called it a manifesto—a public declaration of his plans—and had two thousand copies of it released in Cuba. He wanted to give the country's land to the peasants who worked it. He wanted his future government to take control of, or nationalize, public services and many industries. Castro also wanted to cut rents and make changes in education and factories. Castro called his plan the July 26th Movement in honor of his 1953 attack on the Moncada army barracks.

After releasing his manifesto, Castro intended to send a small group of guerrillas, including Guevara and himself, to invade Cuba. They would fight the government's soldiers in short battles in the mountains. Castro also had supporters in Cuba who were recruiting a network of people in the cities and the mountains to back up the small band of rebels.

This is a rare photo of Guevara (second from left) *and Castro* (right) *at their secret camp near the Cuban coast in 1957.*

Chapter **FOUR**

REVOLUTION

ON NOVEMBER 25, 1956, CHE GUEVARA, FIDEL Castro, and eighty other men set sail for Cuba aboard a 38-foot (11-meter) yacht named *Granma*. (Castro bought the boat from an American, who had likely named it for a grandmother.) The trip was expected to take five days. Instead, it lasted seven. Most of the men got seasick. They ran out of food. The yacht hit a sandbar. Nothing was going as planned.

Before Castro reached Cuba, Batista's government learned that the rebels were coming. One of the rebels probably was a spy. A government official in Cuba held a news conference mocking Castro's plans. The army increased patrols along the coast in Oriente Province, where Castro planned to land.

CUBA: A SHORT HISTORY

Christopher Columbus called the island of Cuba "the most beautiful land that human eyes have ever seen." The name *Cuba* means "central place." The island's location, just 90 miles (144 km) south of Florida, has long attracted other countries, who have tried to control it. From the early 1500s to the early 1900s, Cuba was a Spanish colony.

In 1898 a U.S. ship, the U.S.S. *Maine*, exploded in the harbor of Havana, Cuba's capital. More than 250 people died. It's not clear who destroyed the ship. The United States, Spain, and Cuba all blamed one another. Americans rallied around the slogan, "Remember the *Maine!*" The United States declared war against Spain in April 1898.

The United States quickly defeated Spain and took control of Cuba. The U.S. government amended, or changed, the Cuban constitution to give the United States the right to build a naval base on the island and control what happened in Cuba. About 15,000 Cubans marched to protest the amendment, called the Platt Amendment. They believed that it made Cuba a U.S. colony. The U.S. general in charge of occupying Cuba held a similar opinion. He wrote to U.S. president Theodore Roosevelt, "There is, of course, little or no independence left [to] Cuba under the Platt Amendment."

In 1902 Cuba became an independent republic. But U.S. companies still controlled much of Cuba's land and resources. Fidel Castro didn't want the United States to have so much power over Cuba's economy or to have a military base on Cuban land.

The United States still has a base at Guantánamo Bay, Cuba. In 2002 the U.S. military began using Guantánamo Bay to house people arrested after the September 11, 2001, terrorist attacks in New York and Washington, D.C. About 750 people from more than forty countries have been detained at the U.S. facility in Cuba.

Castro intended to have the rebels aboard the *Granma* join forces with one hundred other supporters in Cuba. They planned to attack a coastal town, then escape to the Sierra Maestra Mountains. Since the *Granma* was two days late, however, Castro's supporters in Cuba had already come and gone. They weren't sure what had happened to the boat. When the *Granma* finally reached the Cuban shore on December 2, things didn't get better. The rebels had to wade a mile (1.6 km) through a thick swamp to reach solid land. Within three days, the Cuban army attacked Castro and his weary men.

Dodging soldiers who were trying to catch them, Guevara and a few other men managed to escape to the thickly forested mountains. The rebels ate the only thing they could find—prickly pear cactus. Of the eighty-two men aboard the *Granma*, fewer than two

Castro and the other Cuban rebels were desperate for food. They ate prickly pear cactus. Both the prickly pear's fruits and its branches, or pads, are edible. But its spines make it difficult to harvest.

dozen managed to regroup. The Cuban army killed the captured rebels.

To avoid the army, Guevara and the others kept moving through the mountains. Some peasants helped feed and hide the rebels. Other peasants told the army where the rebels were hiding. The army caught a few more rebels. By December 21, almost three weeks after landing in Cuba, Guevara and other rebels reunited with Fidel Castro in the Sierra Maestra.

Only about fifteen of the original *Granma* rebels were still free. And they had only a handful of weapons among them. The rebels had left the rest of their guns behind as the army approached. Castro was furious that his troops had ditched their weapons.

But soon the rebels had new guns, thanks to a July 26th Movement supporter named Celia Sánchez. She helped supply Castro and his rebels and became a key figure in the revolutionary movement. On January 17, 1957, the rebels attacked a police barracks in La Plata, a village in the Sierra Maestra. The rebels seized rifles and ammunition and killed two guards. The victory gave the rebels confidence to move forward.

Although the guerrillas were on the move, Guevara still managed to write to his family in Argentina and to his wife and daughter in Mexico. He signed his short notes to his family using his childhood nickname, Tete. Guevara was known as one of the rebel leaders. So, in Cuba he used a fake name—Tete Calvache—to make it harder for the army to catch him.

Celia Sánchez (left) *joins Raúl Castro (Fidel's brother) and Che Guevara* (right) *on a viewing stand during a July 26th Movement celebration in Cuba.*

Soon Guevara and the other rebels skirmished again with local soldiers. This time Guevara shot and killed a man. He wrote Hilda about being "here in the Cuban jungle, alive and thirsting for blood. . . . I am writing this letter over a tin plate with a gun at my side and something new, a cigar in my mouth."

Guevara gained a reputation as a fierce fighter who sought out danger and hated cowards and spies. When the rebels found three men spying on them for the army, Guevara urged Castro to kill the spies. Instead, Castro sent them back to their commander with a warning letter. Guevara later volunteered to shoot a rebel who tried to desert (leave) Castro's guerrilla army.

BEARDS AND HATS

The rebels spent two years in the Sierra Maestra. They worked patiently, building their strength and recruiting more peasants and other supporters. The guerrillas sneaked up on army soldiers, attacked, then quickly hid back in the densely forested mountains.

The peasants called the rebels *barudos,* meaning "the bearded ones." The guerrillas didn't have the time or resources to shave. Guevara himself didn't have much of a beard. One journalist wrote that Guevara's chin had "a few hairs that hoped to form a beard."

For a time, Guevara wore a cap that had belonged to a friend and fellow fighter, Ciro Redondo, who died early in the war. Another rebel recalled, "The cap was a disaster. . . . it was dirty, but because it had belonged to [Ciro] it was what he wanted to wear. Che was a man who was both hard and extraordinarily sentimental." After Guevara lost Ciro's cap, he began wearing a beret, a round, soft, flat hat without a visor. Over time the beret became a symbol of Che.

Life in the mountains was difficult. The rebels traveled often and lived on a simple diet of mostly vegetables. They learned to travel light, setting up rough camps where they could.

Guevara often had trouble breathing. The humid conditions made his asthma worse. Sometimes his asthma was so bad that fellow rebels had to carry him. One day it took Guevara five hours to climb a hill that others climbed in an hour. Another time, Guevara had been struggling to breathe for days. Castro paid a peasant to find medicine. It took two days for the peasant to bring back the medicine. Guevara was too weak to move. Smoking is unhealthy, especially for people with asthma. Yet Guevara insisted that cigars helped him breathe better. He often kept his uniform shirt unbuttoned, saying it was easier for him to breathe with his chest exposed.

Guevara made use of his medical skills while in the mountains. Even though he was mainly a soldier, Guevara still found time to treat some of the local peasants. Doing so confirmed his belief in the need for revolution. He wrote about seeing "prematurely aged and toothless women, children with distended [swollen] bellies [who were starving]." He noted, "We began to feel in our flesh and blood the need for a [major] change in the life of the people. The idea of [agrarian] reform became clear, and oneness with the people ceased being theory and was converted into a fundamental part of our being."

COMMUNIST COMANDANTE

As Castro's revolt grew, so did Guevara's role. By 1957 Castro had two hundred fighters. That June he put Guevara in charge of seventy-five rebels. With a new title, Comandante of the Fourth Column, he was the second-highest-ranking guerrilla. Only Castro himself had more power. Guevara wrote, "It made me feel like the proudest man on earth that day." (The guerrillas had just two columns, or groupings, of troops. But they called Guevara's troops the Fourth Column to trick Batista's army into thinking the rebel group was larger.)

Despite his title, Guevara didn't allow himself special privileges. He camped and ate the same way his soldiers did. Books were his one treat. His family sent him a vintage three-volume set of Jules Verne's complete works. Although Guevara was busy, he always found time to read and write.

Besides keeping a diary, he began writing columns for *El Cuban Libre (The Free Cuban)*, the rebels' newspaper. The paper kept Cubans who lived in cities informed about what was happening to the guerrillas

Jules Verne (1828–1905) was one of Guevara's favorite authors. Verne wrote adventure stories, including A Journey to the Center of the Earth *and* Twenty Thousand Leagues Under the Sea.

in the mountains. Guevara, who never seemed to run out of nicknames, used yet another name for the newspaper. His pen name was Francotirador, or "Sharpshooter." The column was titled, "With an Unloaded Gun." Guevara wrote about his fellow rebels, their revolution, and other struggles around the world. He also wrote a sad story called "The Murdered Puppy," about a friendly dog who was the rebels' mascot. Guevara loved dogs and often had one as a pet. One day the rebels' dog began barking as they tried to sneak up on the enemy. Guevara didn't want the army soldiers to find his men, so he ordered another rebel to strangle the dog. That night as the rebels camped at an abandoned village, another dog came up to befriend them. Guevara wrote, "There, in our presence, with its mild, mischievous and slightly reproachful gaze, observing us through the eyes of another dog, was the murdered puppy."

A front-page *New York Times* article in 1957 did far more than the little rebel newspaper to let people know about Castro and his July 26th Movement. The article noted, "From the looks of things, General Batista cannot possibly hope to suppress the Castro revolt."

Guevara (right) *sits next to Raúl Castro in the rebels' camp.*

Many rumors swirled about why a middle-class Argentinean would choose to fight in Cuba's revolution. Guevara told an Argentinean journalist, "I consider that not only Argentina but all of Latin America is my country."

In March 1958, a newspaper published by the Cuban Communist Party ran a story called "Why Our Party Supports the Sierra Maestra." (Sierra Maestra was another name for Castro's rebel movement.) Castro worried that having Communist supporters would hurt his chances of success. At this point in the campaign, Castro never spoke about Communism. He didn't want to lose supporters who liked him but feared Communism. Guevara kept quiet about his views about Communism.

REBELS IN LOVE

In November 1958, Guevara met a young rebel named Aleida March. She came to Guevara's camp to deliver a message. When she learned that her home in Santa Clara had been raided, March realized she couldn't go back there. She asked Guevara if she could stay in the camp. At first he said no. The comandante didn't like having women stay with his soldiers. Soon, however, Guevara said yes to the twenty-four-year-old March. One night when she couldn't sleep and was sitting outside, Guevara invited her to go along on a raid. "And from that moment on, I never left his side—or let him out of my sight," March said. (Guevara was still married to Hilda Gadea, who was living in Peru with their daughter, Hildita.)

In the battle to conquer Santa Clara, Cuba, Guevara ordered rebel soldiers to destroy the railroad by digging up the tracks.

In December 1958, Guevara and his forces marched to Santa Clara, a city in central Cuba. The guerrillas wanted to take control of the city to divide the island in two. President Batista's government still dominated the capital, Havana, on the island's western side. But if Guevara could win Santa Clara, the rebels would gain an important step toward control of the whole island.

During this key period in the guerrilla war, Guevara realized that he was in love with March. In the middle of the fight for Santa Clara, she rushed out into the street. Guevara said later that seeing her in the battle made him panic. He couldn't calm down until he knew she was safe.

The year ended on a good note for the rebels. Guevara and his troops drove Batista's army out of Santa Clara. The new year began even better. On January 1, 1959, Batista fled Cuba. The dictator realized that he could no longer hold on to his power. But when he flew to nearby Dominican Republic, he did manage to take about $300 million with him. Castro and his rebels had defeated the dictator and prepared to take charge of Cuba.

Guevara (front right), *Castro* (center left), *and Camilo Cienfuego* (back top), *another rebel leader, pass through a crowd in Havana in 1959.*

Chapter **FIVE**

RUNNING A COUNTRY

BY JANUARY 2, 1959, GUEVARA AND HIS TROOPS were on the road, driving to Havana. Along the way, people greeted them as heroes. Guevara's job was to secure La Cabaña, a fortress in Havana built by the Spaniards in the late eighteenth century. Another rebel leader, Camilo Cienfuegos, advanced on Camp Columbia, the country's largest military fortress, also in Havana. Castro was at the south end of the island, in Cuba's second-largest city, Santiago de Cuba.

Early on January 3, 1959, Guevara and his rebels arrived at La Cabaña. Three thousand army soldiers there had already surrendered. Throughout the capital city, the rebels quickly took charge. Citizens and rebels celebrated in the streets.

Castro (top center), *arrives to take over Havana, Cuba, in 1959. Guevara arrived separately.*

Cubans recognized Guevara as a key figure in their revolution. They had read his Sharpshooter articles and followed the progress of the guerrilla war for two years. As one Cuban remarked, "[Guevara] was already a legend. To actually see him for many Cubans was like a vision; you rubbed your eyes. He was physically imposing too, with very white skin, chestnut-colored hair, and he was very attractive."

Supreme Prosecutor

By February 16, Castro was running the country. The new constitution granted citizenship to anyone who had been a rebel comandante for at least a year— which meant that Guevara was legally a Cuban citizen. Castro put him in charge of training the armed forces. Guevara also served as the supreme prosecutor, who oversaw hundreds of quick trials of people suspected of supporting Batista.

About eight hundred people were imprisoned at La Cabaña. Most were soldiers or police, but some prisoners were businesspeople and journalists. As supreme prosecutor, Guevara had to decide whether prisoners deserved to die. He earned a reputation for being cold-blooded. He didn't attend hearings or meet with anyone who was to be executed. Instead, he simply looked at the written records and passed judgment. It's not clear exactly how many executions Guevara ordered—estimates range from two hundred to seven hundred.

Executing Batista supporters and organizing the troops kept Guevara busy. But he also made time to write about the lessons he had learned from the revolution. He began writing a how-to manual for revolutionaries, called *Guerrilla Warfare: A Method*. Guevara often worked fifteen-hour days.

One of the major goals of the revolution was to change the traditional system of land ownership and farming. In this system, a few wealthy landowners or companies profited from the work of many poor peasants. Guevara took the lead in organizing the National Institute for Agrarian Reform (abbreviated in Spanish as INRA). In May 1959, Castro's government passed its first agrarian reform law, giving the government control over about one-third of the country's farm-land. The government seized big and medium-sized privately owned farms and ranches and turned them into state (government-run) farms.

Peasants still lived and worked on the farms. But under Castro's system, they received a salary and a small share in the farm's profits. Many wealthier Cubans whose land was seized left the island and emigrated to the United States.

A Flood of Cubans Heads North

s Castro began to take over privately owned businesses, many middle- and upper-class Cubans fled the country. Most went to the United States and settled in Florida. By the spring of 1960, about sixty thousand Cubans had left the country. Most of them were educated and owned property.

Many of the Cuban exiles (citizens who leave or are forced to leave their country) banded together to overthrow Castro's government. They wanted to reclaim the property they believed was wrongly taken from them. The U.S. government helped train and fund Cubans who wanted to invade Cuba and force Castro out of power.

Within the first ten years of the revolution, half a million Cubans left the island. As the years continued, even more fled Castro's Cuba. The United States still opens its doors to twenty thousand Cubans each year.

Guevara listens attentively to one of Castro's speeches in Havana in the 1960s.

Guevara and Castro believed that more agrarian reforms were needed. Cuba was the world's leading supplier of sugar. But the country didn't grow enough other kinds of food, so Cuba had to trade sugar to buy food and materials. About 70 percent of Cuban sugar ended up in the United States. Meanwhile, most of Cuba's imported goods came from the United States.

Aside from sugar, Cuba's other big moneymaker was tourism. Americans and people from other countries visited Cuban beaches and gambled in the country's casinos. Guevara didn't want to rely on the United States to buy its sugar and supply tourists. He wanted

Cuba to be more self-sufficient. He wanted the country to develop its own industries, with factories that could produce items that Cubans needed and wanted.

NEW COUNTRY, NEW MARRIAGE

After the rebels were settled in Havana and running the country, some parts of life returned to normal. Guevara's wife, Hilda, and their daughter moved to Cuba. Guevara quickly told Hilda that he didn't want to be married to her anymore. The couple divorced on May 22, 1959. Four-year-old Hildita regularly saw her father at his INRA office, where he spent most of his days and nights. Aleida March was his secretary. On June 2, Che and Aleida were married. Guevara wore neatly ironed army fatigues, a change from his usual rumpled and untucked appearance.

Less than two weeks after marrying March, Guevara left Cuba for a three-month world tour. Castro encouraged him to bring his new wife. But Guevara didn't want people to think that he was taking a honeymoon on government money. He visited more than a dozen countries, including Egypt, Pakistan, and the Union of Soviet Socialist Republics (USSR), or Soviet Union. Guevara's goal was to find new trading partners for Cuba. Since the United States opposed the Cuban revolution, Castro and Guevara wanted to find new markets. Within months, Japan, Indonesia, and Egypt established diplomatic and trade ties with Cuba.

Guevara (center front) **married his second wife, Aleida March** (fourth from right) **on June 2, 1959.**

Guevara wrote his mother that touring countries as an official wasn't as much fun as hitchhiking. He wanted to sit and daydream by a pyramid. Instead, he spent his time talking politics and economics with other officials. In the same letter to his mother, Guevara wrote about feeling called to a "historic duty" that was more important than personal relationships:

> I have no home, no woman, no children, nor parents, nor brothers and sisters, my friends are my friends as long as they think politically like I do and yet I am content, I feel something in life, not just a powerful internal strength, which I always felt, but also the power to inject others, and an absolute fatalistic sense of my mission which strips me of all fear.

When Guevara returned to Cuba, he set to work overseeing the country's reforms. He and Castro radically changed the way Cuba was run. They created a central planning board that controlled the country's economy, similar to the way Communist countries such as the Soviet Union worked. This system was very different from the free-market economies of the United States and other Western countries. In a free-market, or capitalist, economy, individual businesses have more freedom to operate as they want and can keep most of the money they earn. Guevara became the key designer of the new Cuban economy. He had no experience in economics or running a country.

In October 1959, a plane carrying Camilo Cienfuegos, one of Guevara's closest comrades from the revolution, disappeared. Guevara wrote, "There has not been a soldier comparable to Camilo." He considered Cienfuegos "the greatest guerrilla leader produced by this revolution." Guevara and other rebels mourned the death of their fellow barudo.

MONEY, SUGAR, AND POWER

In November 1959, Castro named Guevara governor of the Cuban National Bank. He was in charge of Cuba's treasury. He signed the country's currency with his famous nickname, Che. Guevara wasn't interested in money for himself, however. He refused to accept the $1,000 monthly bank salary. He was content to earn $250 a month for being a comandante.

In January 1960, Castro's government took control of all remaining privately owned large farms and plantations. Guevara and Castro viewed sugarcane and other crops as Cuban resources that should belong to all Cubans. The leaders believed that the government had the right to nationalize private property. The Cuban government also nationalized many big businesses, banks, and even some small businesses that were owned privately by Cubans.

A few months later, Cuba got a big boost when the Soviet Union officially established ties with Castro's government. As Cuba grew closer to the Soviet Union, the U.S. government became increasingly concerned about what it saw as Cuba's slide toward Communism.

Starting in June 1960, Cuba took over some oil refineries in Cuba that belonged to U.S. and British oil companies. In July the United States responded by refusing to buy Cuban sugar. The Soviet Union quickly agreed to buy 700,000 tons of sugar a year. In October the United States began a partial embargo of Cuban goods. A trade embargo is an official ban on the sale of goods between two countries. The Soviets agreed to lend Cuba money so it could buy machines and build factories to meet Guevara's goal of fostering more industry within Cuba.

THE COLD WAR

The United States and the Soviet Union had been allies fighting together during World War II. But when the war ended in 1945, the two countries began to square off. After the war, Western democracies, including the United States, formed an alliance known as the North Atlantic Treaty Organization (NATO), while the Soviet Union led the Warsaw Pact, an alliance between the Soviet Union and countries in Eastern Europe that had been taken over by the Soviets.

The political, economic, and ideological conflicts between these two alliances became known as the Cold War. Although it was mostly a war of words, the Cold War led to a buildup of weapons in the United States and the Soviet Union. These two nations were the world's superpowers—big countries with powerful militaries and many resources. The superpowers also held very different views of how the world should be. The United States wanted to spread democracy and allow capitalism to flourish. The Soviet Union wanted to spread Communism.

This rivalry spurred both nations to spend huge amounts of money building weapons—a competition known as the arms race. By the late 1950s, both the United States and the Soviet Union had built enough nuclear bombs to completely destroy one another—and possibly the whole world with them. Both sides believed that missiles were the key to winning a nuclear war.

One of the flashpoints of the Cold War occurred in October 1962. That year the United States discovered that the Soviet Union was installing nuclear missile bases in Cuba, in striking range of the United States. The confrontation, known as the Cuban missile crisis, lasted seven days before leaders of the two nations reached an agreement that averted a nuclear showdown.

Despite some periods of relaxation and cooperation, the Cold War did not end until the late 1980s. In that era, the Soviet Union and Communism in the East collapsed.

In October Guevara began another world tour to rally countries to support Cuba. This time he visited Eastern European countries, including East Germany and Czechoslovakia, as well as the Soviet Union and China, another Communist nation. Guevara met with Soviet prime minister Nikita Khrushchev and Chinese leader Mao Zedong. While Che was in China, Aleida gave birth to their first child, a girl named Aleidita, on November 24.

Back in Cuba, some citizens who had supported the revolution were concerned about Castro's ties to Soviet Communists. Even though Castro and Guevara did not call their government Communist, they were enacting Communist-style laws and reforms. More Cubans began criticizing Castro's government. To stop students and teachers from speaking out and protesting, the government took control of the country's leading university in Havana. Castro also began closing newspapers and TV stations that were critical of him or of Communism. By the end of 1960, the Cuban government had set up a work camp. People who opposed the government were forced to do hard labor there.

U.S. president John F. Kennedy (left) *and the previous president, Dwight Eisenhower* (right) *meet at the White House. Their decisions about U.S. relations with Cuba greatly affected Guevara's life.*

Chapter **SIX**

TWO SUPERPOWERS, ONE SMALL ISLAND

BY **1961** RELATIONS BETWEEN THE UNITED STATES and Cuba were quickly getting worse. On January 3, 1961, shortly before the end of his term as president, Dwight D. Eisenhower made one last important decision. He ordered U.S. diplomats to cut ties with Cuba. The two countries seemed headed toward war. When John F. Kennedy entered the White House, he extended the trade restrictions against Cuba, further limiting what items the two countries could buy or sell to each other. (Kennedy reportedly asked an aide to buy thousands of Cuban cigars, which Kennedy liked, just before the trade embargo started.)

In February 1961, Guevara gained yet another new title—minister of industries. He encouraged Cubans to volunteer their time to help their country by doing manual labor. In China Guevara had been impressed by Mao's volunteer work brigades. (Both China and Cuba relied on volunteer workers. But it's questionable how voluntary the programs were. When officials such as Guevara told their staffers to volunteer, they likely didn't have much choice but to do so.)

Guevara believed in volunteering and made an example of himself. He worked long hours at his office Monday through Saturday helping to run the country. On Sunday, his only day off, he volunteered doing physical labor. Various pictures show him shirtless, lifting a heavy sack at a dock. At a construction site, he is behind the wheel of a construction vehicle with his face covered in grime or helping to haul a slab of concrete. A famous photograph called "Muddy Boots" shows Guevara with his boots spattered, shirt unbuttoned, and beret tipped back. He looks happy and relaxed.

Guevara wasn't close to many people. But he stayed in touch with some old friends, including Alberto Granado, his motorcycle-traveling companion. In March 1961, Granado and his family moved to Cuba, where Granado began working as a medical school professor in Havana.

THE BAY OF PIGS

U.S. businesses, which had owned a large share of Cuba's resources, felt threatened by Castro's revolution. One historian wrote, "American companies controlled 80 to 100 percent of Cuba's utilities, mines, cattle

COVERING THE REVOLUTION

The famous "Muddy Boots" photo of Che Guevara was taken by a father-son team, Osvaldo and Roberto Salas. They made a life of documenting the Cuban revolution. Osvaldo was chief of photography for the *Revolución* newspaper. His son, Roberto, was one of Castro's personal photographers. Both photographers had access to Castro, Guevara, and other Cuban leaders.

Roberto Salas said that one of his favorite pictures was the first one he took of Guevara and Castro. It was about two weeks after the rebels had reached Havana. In the middle of the night, Castro and Guevara were talking in a dark room in the presidential estate, later renamed the Palace of the Revolution. The dramatic black-and-white photo shows Guevara leaning up to Castro, helping the Cuban leader light his cigar. Guevara looks young and passionate.

Roberto Salas said he considered Guevara "the most intense guy I ever met, always kind of an outsider. . . . Che always felt like he had a hard time fitting in. And he was always obsessed by thinking about the revolutionary struggle. Che was great about analyzing global and political situations. But he wasn't a good judge of character, and I think he knew it."

ranches, and oil refineries, 40 percent of the sugar industry, and 50 percent of the public railways." Castro's government seized more than 1 million acres (405,000 hectares) of land that belonged to U.S. companies.

President Kennedy wanted to protect U.S. business interests in Cuba and other parts of Latin America. On April 3, 1961, a White House report noted that Cuba posed a "clear and present danger" to the United States and Central and South America. Still, Kennedy publicly stated on April 13, "There will not be, under any conditions, any intervention in Cuba by the United States armed forces."

Two days later, on April 15, 1961, several U.S. B-26 bomber planes disguised to look like Cuban air force planes attacked military airfields at Havana and Santiago de Cuba. In one morning, five of the Cuban air force's thirteen planes were wiped out. At a funeral for the pilots, Castro for the first time said that Cuba was a Socialist country. Socialism is a political and economic theory based on the idea that society as a whole, rather than individuals, should control a country's resources. Communism is a form of Socialism. When Castro described Cuba as a Socialist country, many Americans feared that it was really Communist.

Then, on April 17, about fifteen thousand Cuban exiles, hoping to overthrow Castro, invaded Cuba. The exiles had support from the Central Intelligence Agency, the U.S. secret intelligence organization. The exiles invaded at a beach known as the Bay of Pigs.

Castro ordered his army to resist the exiles' attack. Guevara oversaw troops at the island's westernmost province, Pinar Del Río. An accident there almost cost him his life. Guevara's pistol slipped from its holster,

Cuban exiles from the United States storm the beach during the Bay of Pigs invasion of Cuba in April 1961.

the gun went off, and a bullet skimmed the side of his face. When medics gave Guevara an antibiotic to prevent infection, he had a bad reaction to the drug and nearly died.

Back at the Bay of Pigs, Castro's army quickly defeated the unorganized exiles. By April 19, two days after the invasion began, almost 1,200 exiles had been captured. The army killed 100 of them, while the exiles were able to kill more than 150 Cuban soldiers. The exiles expected Cubans to join them in forcing Castro out, but that didn't happen. The exiles also thought the United States would send more troops and air force support. But President Kennedy didn't want to send

U.S. troops and risk a war against Cuba and its strong supporter, the Soviet Union.

After his Bay of Pigs victory, Castro had 1,200 prisoners of war—and new power to bargain with the United States. After negotiations, the United States sent Cuba more than sixty million dollars' worth of food and medicine. In exchange, Castro sent the captured Cuban exiles back to the United States.

Meanwhile, the United States pressured other countries in Central and South America to cut ties with Castro. By December 1961, Colombia, Nicaragua, Panama, and Costa Rica were among the nations that had cut off relations with the Socialist country. Only Mexico remained open to trade with Cuba.

TOTAL EMBARGO

In February 1962, the United States ordered a total trade embargo with Cuba, meaning that it would no longer buy anything from or sell anything to Cuba. The United States also threatened to cut off aid to any country that continued to trade with Cuba. The island nation was being cut off from its neighbors.

After the embargo, Cuba began rationing food and other goods. Citizens received a limited number of coupons that they could use to buy items such as food and clothing. The rations of basic groceries such as rice and beans were supposed to last a month. But they only lasted most people a week or so. Many Cubans nearly starved.

The embargo made life harder for all Cubans, including Guevara and his family. Since Guevara accepted only part of the salary he was entitled to, his family often struggled to make ends meet. Guevara's bodyguards gave Aleida some of their own money because she didn't have enough to buy food for the family. Guevara needed bodyguards because assassins had tried to kill him on more than one occasion. One time, while Guevara was giving a speech in Uruguay, South America, a gun went off and killed a member of the audience. Guevara's bodyguard said the bullet was meant for Che.

In May 1962, Che and Aleida's second child was born. Camilo was Guevara's first son. Guevara's family was growing, but that didn't mean he had more time to spend at home. He was still focused on trying to make Cuba succeed. He also wanted to nurture rebellion elsewhere.

Guevara hoped to start a revolution in Argentina. He began to quietly recruit some of his countrymen to come to Cuba to train as guerrillas. He sent his friend Alberto Granado back to Argentina to find recruits. Guevara told the Argentineans who joined him, "From this moment on, consider yourself dead. Death is the only certainty in this; some of you may survive, but all of you should consider what remains of your lives as borrowed time."

In late summer, Guevara traveled again to the Soviet Union. He was looking for help finding countries willing to trade with Cuba. Cubans were hungry. Guevara's plan to industrialize the country wasn't paying off.

THE CUBAN MISSILE CRISIS

In mid-October 1962, a U.S. spy plane spotted Soviet missiles in Cuba. Workers were putting nuclear warheads on sixty Soviet missiles that could be fired against the United States. On October 22, President Kennedy went on television to tell Americans about the situation.

Kennedy announced a U.S. military blockade to prevent any ships or airplanes from reaching Cuba. He also said that the United States would go to war if necessary. Soviet premier Khrushchev warned that such action could lead to "catastrophic consequences for world peace." The Soviets said they put the missiles in Cuba to protect the island from U.S. aggression. For thirteen days in October, the world watched as the two superpowers edged toward nuclear war over Cuba.

In Cuba Castro also prepared for war. Guevara was in charge of guerrilla troops, including some recruited from Argentina. Guevara and his soldiers were based in a cave on the island's west end, near one of the Soviet missile sites.

But on October 28, without consulting the Cubans, Khrushchev made a deal with President Kennedy. The Soviets agreed to dismantle their missiles in Cuba if the United States would remove its missiles in Turkey, a country close to the Soviet Union. Khrushchev also got the United States to agree not to attack Cuba. Khrushchev supposedly said, "We are face to face with the danger of war and nuclear catastrophe. In order to save the world we must retreat."

Castro and Guevara were enraged that the Soviets negotiated with the Americans without consulting Cuba. The Cuban missile crisis didn't lead to nuclear war. But for Guevara, the battle wasn't over. He intended to bring Cuba's revolution to other countries, whatever the consequences.

Guevara (front, second from left) ***greets Communist Chinese diplomats arriving at the Havana airport on March 8, 1961.***

Chapter **SEVEN**

THE NEW MAN

CHE GUEVARA CONTINUED TO SEARCH FOR WAYS TO make Cuba thrive. He was convinced of the need for a "New Man," one who would put the interests of the country ahead of personal interests.

But it wasn't easy to build a new man or a new woman, and it wasn't easy to change Cuba's economy. Guevara was still trying to shift Cuba from farming to industry, but the small island didn't have enough machinery and goods. The U.S. trade embargo against Cuba didn't help. And the Cuban missile crisis had damaged relations between Cuba and the Soviet Union.

Guevara began to lose faith in the Soviets. He preferred the Chinese model of Communism rather than

the Soviet way. Still, Guevara remained a firm supporter of Communism, as did Castro. In December
1962, Castro declared himself to be a Marxist-Leninist.
He believed in the Communist theories of Karl Marx
and Vladimir Lenin. Lenin was a leader of the 1917
Russian Revolution that led to the creation of the
Soviet Union. He put his own mark on the
theories of Karl Marx, a German political writer.

Castro continued to work with the Soviets, but as
Guevara grew more critical of them, he lost influence
within the government. At the same time, Guevara's
ideas for transforming Cuba were not working. One
critic noted that when Guevara was in charge of the
Cuban economy, sugar production nearly collapsed.

FROM OXEN TO TRACTORS AND BACK

The Soviet Union sent many items to Cuba to help the
struggling island. But the Soviet tractors and cars
didn't last long. When the Soviet-made machines
broke, the Cubans didn't have parts to fix them.

For decades, Cuban farmers had used oxen in their
fields to help plant and harvest their crops. In the early 1960s,
farmers got the chance to modernize their operations. Instead of
oxen, they had Soviet tractors. When the tractors broke, the
farmers had to go back to using oxen to bring in their crops.

The plan to create more industry failed and rationing was introduced. These policy failures, coupled with the U.S. embargo, led to severe food shortages and widespread hunger throughout Cuba. Guevara blamed the U.S. embargo for many of Cuba's struggles.

While Guevara tackled large-scale problems at work, at home he had cause for celebration. On his thirty-fifth birthday, June 14, 1963, Guevara became a father again. Aleida gave birth to a baby girl, named Celia for Che's mother.

LEAVING CUBA

In July 1963, Guevara traveled to Algeria to celebrate the North African nation's first anniversary of independence from French rule. In a speech there, Guevara admitted that his way of changing Cuba had failed. He had tried to create a centralized economy that the government could control. Workers were supposed to be willing to sacrifice their needs for the good of the country. But that hadn't happened.

Castro, too, believed that Guevara had failed. He decided that Guevara should no longer be in charge of Cuba's economy, especially the crucial sugar crop. Guevara was given more ceremonial jobs, such as representing Cuba at trade conferences and other events. The effort to change Cuban society had taken a toll on Guevara. A journalist wrote, "Che was not a desk-man: he was a creator of revolutions, and it was apparent; he was not, or was in spite of himself, an administrator. Somehow, that tension of a caged lion that was his apparent calm betrayed had to explode. He needed the sierra."

The lion who was meant for revolution needed to find a way out of his cage of administrative duties. He thought about how to change society. Guevara wanted to liberate poor people in other parts of Latin America and in Africa. He wanted to spread revolution to other countries.

In 1964 Castro signed a deal with the Soviet Union that upset Guevara. Castro said that Cuba would not provide help to revolutionary movements in Latin America. The Soviets didn't want another episode like the Cuban missile crisis. They wanted to maintain peace with the United States. That meant not encouraging the spread of Socialism and Communism in Latin America.

On December 11, 1964, Guevara gave an impassioned speech at the United Nations in New York. (Cuba had been a member of the United Nations since 1945.) He talked about the need for revolutions to wipe out imperialism, the power or influence of one nation over others. Guevara saw the United States as an imperialist country that was trying to build an empire and extend its influence throughout the world. When the speech was over, Guevara left New York and flew to Africa. He began a three-month journey, getting to know the continent. He also made brief trips to China and Europe.

During a visit to Paris, France, Guevara met Laurent Kabila. Kabila was trying to organize a revolution in the Congo, a big country in central Africa that had been a Belgian colony. The Congo had become an independent country in 1960. But Belgians still controlled Congo's military and didn't want the Congolese people to run their own country. (Congo has also been known as Zaire or the Belgian Congo. In 1997 the country's official name became Democratic Republic of the Congo.)

While he was in Africa, Guevara became a father for the fifth time. Once again, he was gone when Aleida gave birth. Their fourth child, a son named Ernesto, was born on February 24, 1965. The next day, Guevara

Guevara holds his infant son, Ernesto. Young Aleidita leans on her father's shoulder.

gave a speech in Algiers, Algeria, that became known in Cuba as "his last bullet." It would be his last big public speech. Guevara spoke about revolutions in poor, underdeveloped countries. He criticized the Soviet Union for not giving free weapons to poor countries.

ANOTHER REVOLUTION

After visiting Africa, Guevara went home to Cuba, but not for long. Soon the revolutionary who had left his parents, siblings, and friends years ago in Argentina would leave his family again. This time Guevara was headed to the Congo to support a pro-Lumumba Marxist movement. Patrice Lumumba had been the country's first prime minister. But in 1961, not long after taking office, he was assassinated. By 1965, a dictator named Mobutu Sese Seko ruled Congo. Mobutu had played a role in Lumumba's murder. Guevara and Kabila wanted to get rid of Mobutu, who was backed by the United States. They wanted Congo to be led by a Marxist.

On April 1, 1965, Guevara left Cuba in disguise. He wore padded clothes and big glasses, shaved his beard, and had a barber pluck his hair so he would look bald. He used a fake name—his passport claimed he was Ramón Benítez. Guevara left behind several letters for his family, as well as one for Fidel Castro. In the letter to Castro, Guevara officially resigned from all his Cuban duties—even his citizenship.

Guevara told Castro that he could make his resignation public whenever the Cuban leader chose. Guevara said he was leaving to fulfill what he called "the most sacred of duties: to fight against imperialism wherever one may be.... If my final hour finds me under other skies, my last thought will be of this people and especially of you."

Guevara's letters to his parents and children were more personal. He said he loved them and admitted that he did not always know how to show his love. He left Aleida a tape of him reading his favorite love poems. He urged his children to "grow up as good revolutionaries." The advice Guevara gave his five children offered a summary of his philosophy:

> Remember that the Revolution is what is important and that each of us, on our own, is worthless. Above all, try always to be able to feel deeply any injustice against any person in any part of the world. It is the most beautiful quality of a revolutionary.
>
> Until always, little children, I still hope to see you again. A really big kiss and a hug from Papa.

The rebels in Congo feared that the famous guerrilla's presence would anger other countries. So Guevara kept his disguise and began using a Swahili nickname, Tatu. He and a small band of other Cubans went to the mountains to quietly join Congo's rebels.

Many of the Cubans, including Guevara, soon became sick. Guevara had a high fever and took weeks to recover. During that time, he learned that his mother Celia was dying. He wrote a ten-page story called "The Stone," describing his sadness about losing his mother. The story mentioned the only two mementos Guevara had brought to Congo—a gauze scarf from his wife and a key chain with a stone from his mother. Unaware that her son was in Africa, Celia died on May 19, 1965.

Guevara (left) *cradles a Congolese child. A Congolese rebel soldier stands next to them in this photograph taken in 1965.*

Most of the world didn't know where Guevara was. Finally, on October 3, 1965, Castro publicly read Guevara's resignation letter, ending months of speculation about his whereabouts.

Guevara realized that the Congo rebellion would not happen quickly. He guessed that it would take more than five years. In a letter to Castro on October 5, 1965, Guevara described the situation: "We are making mistakes that may prove very costly. . . . There are too many armed men; what is lacking are soldiers. . . . We cannot liberate by ourselves a country that does not want to fight." The Congolese rebels were disorganized, and the leaders wanted to control their own fight for independence, without Guevara's participation.

By December, eight months after he arrived, Guevara was forced to give up. He retreated to an East African country, Tanzania, where he stayed in hiding for several months. He wrote about his experience in Africa. "This is the history of a failure," he wrote bluntly. His Africa dream had turned into a nightmare. Guevara needed to find another place to go. He wanted to be part of another revolution, closer to home back in Latin America.

Reluctant to return to Cuba and banned from Argentina, Guevara went to Bolivia in 1966. He tried to start a revolution there.

Chapter **EIGHT**

BOLIVIA AND BEYOND

CHE **G**UEVARA **FELT LIKE A MAN WITHOUT A COUNTRY.**
He didn't want to go back to Cuba, where he would
have another desk job. He wanted to return to
Argentina. But the military government opposed him,
and even the Communist Party there didn't want him.
The Argentinean Communist leaders probably feared
that if Guevara returned to their country, he would
take their power.

Since he wasn't welcome back home, Guevara
decided to at least get close to Argentina. By mid-
1966, Guevara was planning another revolution. The
setting this time was Bolivia, one of Argentina's neighbors. Before he left for Bolivia, Guevara spent a little
time back in Cuba. He had a final dinner with Fidel

Castro. The two men talked all night, then hugged good-bye. Guevara was still in disguise, clean-shaven with a receding hairline. Guevara's children didn't recognize him. He went to see them, pretending to be Uncle Ramón. It was the last time Aleida and the children saw Guevara.

In November 1966, pretending to be a Uruguayan businessman named Adolfo Mena González, Guevara went to Bolivia. "I've come to stay," he said, "And the only way that I will leave here is dead, or crossing a

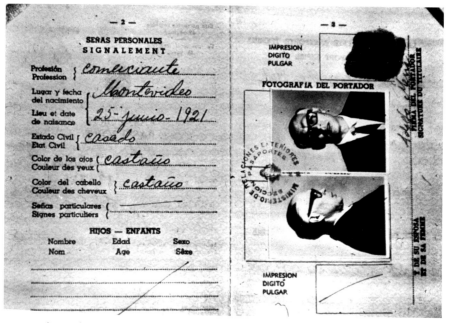

The Bolivian Embassy in Washington, D.C., identified this as the forged passport Guevara used to enter Bolivia in 1966.

border, shooting bullets as I go." Guevara hoped that a guerrilla war in Bolivia would ignite other Latin American rebellions. But even though a few Communists let Guevara use their land to train, the famous revolutionary wasn't welcome in Bolivia. The country's president, René Barrientos, supposedly said he wanted to see Guevara's head on a pike (spear). The Bolivian government was getting help from the United States, which sent advisers to train the Bolivian army. Guevara's presence might endanger that aid.

Nevertheless, Guevara led about two dozen guerrillas, mostly Cubans who had been with him for years. Unlike the Cuban guerrilla movement years earlier in the Sierra Maestra, Guevara's fighters in Bolivia didn't have backup. They didn't have supporters in the city, nor did they have peasants helping them in the mountains. Bolivia's Communist Party supported the Soviet style of Communism rather than the Chinese model that Guevara favored. Guevara's small group was on its own, surrounded by peasants who didn't trust the guerrillas and government soldiers trying to defeat them.

The Bolivian soldiers had help. The U.S. Central Intelligence Agency was also trying to track down Guevara's troops. The United States worried that if Guevara led another successful revolution, other Latin American countries would also become Communist.

In April 1967, Guevara released a public statement, trying to inspire revolutions around the globe. He discussed Vietnam, the Southeast Asian country at the center of a long power struggle involving numerous countries. France and later the United States spent years trying to control Vietnam. "The people of three continents focus their attention on Vietnam and learn their lesson," Guevara wrote. He encouraged more countries to be like Vietnam and fight to the death against what he called "the great enemy of mankind: the United States of America."

Guevara warned of a "cruel war" against imperialism: "How close we could look into a bright future should two, three, or many Vietnams flourish throughout the world with their share of deaths and their immense tragedies."

SICKNESS AND FAILURE

As he approached the age of forty, Guevara still had a passion for revolution. But his body was worn out. He was too sick to fight. His asthma worsened in the Bolivian mountains, and he suffered other health problems as well. Often he was so weak he had to ride on a mule. His men had little food and ended up eating most of their horses and mules. But Guevara refused to let them kill his mule. One time he was so weak from vomiting and diarrhea that his men had to carry him in a hammock. On June 14, 1967, Guevara's thirty-ninth birthday, he wrote in his journal, "I am inevitably approaching the age when my future as a guerrilla must be considered. For now, I'm still in one piece."

In one of the last photos taken of Guevara, he poses with his mule Chico in Bolivia.

He and his men were on the move constantly, ducking and fighting, trying to stay ahead of the Bolivian soldiers. The Bolivian government dropped pamphlets in the mountains. They showed a cartoon of a beret-clad guerrilla on a mule being chased by a big bayonet (a weapon that has a blade attached to a rifle). The caption read, "EL FIN DEL CHE"—the end of Che.

As the months of guerrilla war dragged on, Guevara lost several of his closest Cuban comrades. Carlos "Tuma" Coello was shot in the liver during a skirmish in June. Guevara held his friend as he died. Later, Guevara wrote, "With his death I have lost an inseparable comrade and companion over all the recent years. His loyalty was unwavering, and I feel his absence almost as if he were my own son."

By fall, Guevara and the twenty or so remaining rebels had reached a remote mountain village. There, on October 8, Bolivian troops captured Che and most of his men. Six guerrillas—three Cuban, three Bolivian—escaped. Guevara was shot in the calf and left unarmed. He was taken captive and tied up on the dirt floor of the village schoolhouse. The bodies of two of his men lay next to him.

Bolivian army officers and a CIA agent flew in to interview the notorious guerrilla. CIA agent Felix Rodríguez described how Guevara looked with his arms and legs tied up and his leg bleeding: "He was a mess. Hair matted, clothes ragged and torn." The next day, the Bolivian army sent orders to kill Che. The CIA agent was a Cuban who had fled the island after Fidel Castro's takeover and spent years fighting Castro's regime. He broke the news to Guevara that he would die. Then Rodríguez hugged his prisoner.

"It was a tremendously emotional moment for me," Rodríguez recalled. "I no longer hated him. His moment of truth had come, and he was conducting himself like a man. He was facing his death with courage and grace."

A Bolivian soldier came to shoot Guevara. Rodríguez told him not to shoot Che in the face. Supposedly Guevara's last words were, "Shoot, coward, you're only going to kill a man." On the afternoon of October 9, 1967, in a secluded mountain village in Bolivia, Ernesto "Che" Guevara died.

The bullet that pierced Guevara's chest did not end Che's story. His body was displayed so people could see that the world's most famous revolutionary had been killed. His body was painfully thin, with a bullet wound visible on his bare chest. Village women cut snippets of Guevara's hair, a keepsake of a man both admired and hated. Bolivian soldiers cut off his hands, then buried his body, along with those of his men, in a secret grave in Vallegrande, Bolivia. Guevara's hands were sent to Cuba so that Castro would have proof that the famous rebel was indeed dead.

Word of Guevara's death spread quickly. Within days, Fidel Castro announced the news to his country. Cuba began three days of mourning. Castro declared October 8, Che's last day of battle, as the Day of the Heroic Guerrilla. In Havana, more than one million people honored the Argentinean who helped shape their country.

Bolivian soldiers and journalists surround Guevara's body. It was on public display in Bolivia after he was shot in October 1967.

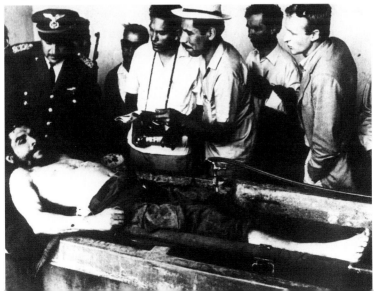

This likeness of Guevara is on a government office building in Havana.

A year after Guevara's death, one of his medical school friends, Tita Infante, wrote a tribute that still resonates today: "Ernesto has died, but he had already been born into eternity."

A LEGEND LIVES

Decades after Che Guevara's death, his legend thrives. A mural covering a five-story building in Havana's Plaza of the Revolution displays a familiar image of Che wearing his beret. Throughout Cuba schoolchildren sing, "Seremos como Che" ("We will be like Che"). The Che Guevara Studies Center in Havana still turns out books and articles about a man who has been dead as long as he lived. In 1997 Guevara's body was recovered from its grave in Bolivia. His remains were taken to Cuba, where he was reburied at Santa Clara, the scene of his key victory.

Ernesto Guevara answered to many names when he was alive, from his youthful nicknames of Chancho (the pig), Fuser (Furious Serna), and El Palao (Baldy) to his wartime names of Tete Calvache and Sharpshooter and the aliases he used while traveling. The CIA's code name for Guevara was Amquack. But Guevara was famous enough to be known by his first name only, Che.

A Guevara memorial and museum mark his final resting place in Santa Clara, Cuba.

Part of Che's enduring appeal stems from when and how his life ended. He died young, as a fighter, not a bureaucrat. One Cuban official noted that Guevara's death in battle set a standard for other Latin American revolutions. "The truth is that his death helped us tremendously," the official said. "It's unlikely we would have had all the revolutionary solidarity we have had over the years if it weren't for Che dying the way he did."

Guevara's image is everywhere in Cuba, on money and stamps, on public murals, and in private homes. But his presence remains strong far beyond his adopted country. His legacy is even a force in the United States, the country he hated. In 2004 viewers flocked to a Spanish movie, *The Motorcycle Diaries*, about Che's youthful

A recording of Castro reading the 1965 resignation letter Guevara left behind when he went to the Congo remains popular in Cuba.

travels. Books, poems, songs, and even a video game tell Guevara's story or some version of it. A character named Che Guevara narrates the popular 1978 theatrical musical (and 1996 movie) *Evita*, even though Che had nothing to do with the Argentinean leaders Evita and Juan Perón.

The Internet search engine Google lists about two million sites linked directly or indirectly to Guevara. One site, http://www.che-lives.com, claims to offer "all your revolutionary needs." Che's face stares out from countless T-shirts and posters, not to mention clocks, backpacks, key chains, lingerie, and hoodies.

Photographer Alberto Korda took the most widely known photo of Guevara—an image of him in his beret. The photo has been reproduced as a huge mural in Havana and on millions of items sold worldwide. The photographer sued a company that used the famous photo to sell vodka. Korda won $70,000 from the company. Guevara's family say they also plan to sue companies that exploit Che's image.

At times the image of Che is used as a joke. A 2004 *New Yorker* cartoon shows Guevara wearing his typical beret and a Simpsons T-shirt. A poster shows Che with a propeller beanie and a T-shirt that reads, "Vote for Pedro," the slogan from *Napoleon Dynamite*, a teen movie released in 2004. Fancy clothing shops in Los Angeles carried cashmere sweaters with Che's image—for $198. And a travel company marketed "In His Footsteps," a tour of key spots in Cuba where Che fought.

Guevara appears on this Cuban coin minted in 1992. It is worth three Cuban pesos (about US$0.04).

ICON

Time magazine ranked Guevara among the one hundred most influential people of the twentieth century. Chilean writer Ariel Dorfman noted that although "the humanity that worships Che has by and large turned away from just about everything he believed in," Guevara's legend lives on because his ideals still have power. Dorfman called Guevara a "secular saint" (a non-religous saint) who could not tolerate a world where so many people are forced to live in poverty, without the basics of food and freedom. But many other people despise Guevara because he wanted to overthrow governments and reshape society.

The *Time* essay ends with a warning: "More than three billion human beings on this planet right now live on less than $2 a day. And every day that breaks, 40,000 children—more than one every second!—succumb to [get] diseases linked to chronic hunger. . . . The powerful of the earth should take heed: deep inside that T shirt where we have tried to trap him, the eyes of Che Guevara are still burning with impatience."

Che Guevara is dead, but the ideas he fought for live on. Millions of poor people across the world struggle to find basic food, shelter, and work. And many people are trying to find ways to overcome those problems. Guevara believed that armed revolution was the best way to help poor people get power. His revolutions mostly failed, but the conditions behind the revolutions remain.

TIMELINE

1928 Ernesto Guevara de la Serna is born in Rosario, Argentina, on June 14.

1947 Guevara begins to study medicine at the University of Buenos Aires.

1950 Guevara and a friend, Alberto Granado, begin a seven-month journey through South America on January 1.

1953 Guevara graduates from medical school in March and becomes a medical doctor. He begins another long trip through South America and ends up in Mexico City.

1955 Guevara marries Hilda Gadea, a Peruvian activist, on August 18. They live in Mexico City.

1956 Hilda gives birth to a daughter, called Hildita, on February 15. In June Mexican police arrest Guevara, Fidel Castro, and other Cubans for planning a rebellion against Cuba. On November 25, Castro, Guevara, and eighty others leave Mexico on board the yacht *Granma*. On December 2, they land in Cuba and within days are attacked. Castro, Guevara, and about fifteen others regroup and hide in the Sierra Maestra Mountains.

1957 Guevara is named Commandante of the Fourth Column.

1958 Guevara and his troops seize the city of Santa Clara on December 31.

1959 President Batista flees Cuba on January 1. The next day, Guevara and other rebels march into Havana and take control of the city. Guevara divorces Hilda Gadea on May 22 and marries Aleida March on June 2. Castro puts Guevara in charge of the country's agrarian reform and the Cuban National Bank.

1960 Guevara's book, *Guerrilla Warfare: A Method*, is published. Guevara visits Eastern European countries, China, the Soviet Union, and North Korea. Cuba begins trade with the Soviet Union.

1961 Guevara is named minister for industry. U.S. airplanes target Cuban military airfields on April 15. With U.S. support, fifteen hundred Cuban exiles invade Cuba at the Bay of Pigs on April 17. Castro's army defeats the exiles within three days.

1962 The United States announces a trade embargo against Cuba in February. The Soviet Union installs missiles in Cuba. The two superpowers almost unleash a nuclear war during the Cuban missile crisis in October. The Soviets negotiate with U.S. president John F. Kennedy to end the crisis.

1964 Guevara speaks at the United Nations in December. That month he flies to Africa to begin three months touring the continent.

1965 Guevara returns to Cuba in March and makes his last public appearances. In April he leaves for the Congo in disguise, after giving Castro his letter of resignation. Guevara spends months failing to organize a guerrilla war in the Congo. He retreats to Tanzania in December.

1966 Guevara organizes guerrillas to fight in Bolivia. He arrives in Bolivia with his rebel troops in November.

1967 Bolivian troops capture Guevara and most of his remaining rebels on October 8. Guevara is executed on October 9. His body is secretly buried in a mass grave with other rebels. Cuba begins three days of mourning on October 15.

1997 Guevara's body is recovered from its grave in Bolivia and returned to Cuba. Guevara is buried with full military honors on July 12 in Santa Clara.

2004 *The Motorcycle Diaries* movie premieres in the United States.

SOURCE NOTES

16   Ernesto Che Guevara, *Self Portrait: Che Guevara*, ed. Victor Casaus, (Melbourne: Ocean Press, 2004), 38.

16   Ibid., 28.

16   Ibid.

20   Jon Lee Anderson, *Che Guevara: A Revolutionary Life* (New York: Grove Press, 1997), 73.

20   Ernesto Che Guevara, *The Motorcycle Diaries: Notes on a Latin American Journey* (Melbourne: Ocean Press, 2003), 35.

21   Ibid., 52.

21   Ibid., 59.

22   Alberto Granado, *Traveling with Che Guevara: The Making of a Revolutionary* (New York: Newmarket Press, 2004), 48.

23   Ibid., 154.

23   Ibid., 70.

24   Guevara, *The Motorcycle Diaries*, 70–71.

24–25   Ibid., 77–78.

27   Granado, *Traveling with Che Guevara*, 123.

27   Anderson, *Che Guevara*, 39.

29   Granado, *Traveling with Che Guevara*, 125–126.

29   Ibid., 126.

34   Anderson, *Che Guevara*, 165.

34 Ibid., 163.
36 Guevara, *Self Portrait*, 103.
37 Anderson, *Che Guevara*, 180.
39 Guevara, *Self Portrait*, 109.
40 Ibid., 104.
44 Jaime Suchlicki, *Cuba: From Columbus to Castro and Beyond*. 5th ed. (Washington, DC: Brassey's Inc., 2002), 1.
44 Kumari Campbell, *Cuba in Pictures* (Minneapolis: Lerner Publications Company, 2005), 4.
44 Howard Zinn, *A People's History of the United States: 1492–Present* (New York: Perennial Classics, 2003), 312.
48 Anderson, *Che Guevara*, 229.
48 Guevara, *Self Portrait*, 120.
49 Anderson, *Che Guevara*, 342.
50 Ibid., 251.
50 Ibid., 268.
52 Guevara, *Self Portrait*, 131.
52 Anderson, *Che Guevara*, 245.
53 Guevara, *Self Portrait*, 124.
53 Anderson, *Che Guevara*, 314–315.
53 Ibid., 361.
55 Osvaldo Salas and Roberto Salas, *Fidel's Cuba: A Revolution in Pictures* (New York: Thunder's Mouth Press; and Hillsboro, OR: Beyond Words Publishing, 1998), 1.
58 Anderson, *Che Guevara*, 381.
63 Ibid., 433.
64 Guevara, *Self Portrait*, 184.
64 Ibid.
71 Salas and Salas, *Fidel's Cuba*, 112.
71 Zinn, *A People's History of the United States*, 439.
72 Ibid., 440.
72 Ibid.
75 Anderson, *Che Guevara*, 543.
76 "Kennedy Goes Public," *The Cuban Missile Crisis: Fourteen Days in October*, 1997, http://www.library.thinkquest.org (August 24, 2005).

77   Richard Reeves, "Thirteen Days in October," *New York Times*, October 8, 1997.

81–82   Anderson, *Che Guevara*, 609.

84   Ibid., 623.

84   "Farewell Letter to Fidel," *Che Lives*, 2004, http://www.che-lives.com (August 12, 2005).

85   Anderson, *Che Guevara*, 634.

85   Ibid.

87   "From Cuba to Congo, Dream to Disaster for Che Guevara," *Guardian*, August 12, 2000, http://www.books.guardian.co.uk (September 12, 2005).

87   Ibid.

90–91   Anderson, *Che Guevara*, 702.

92   "Message to the Tricontinental," *Che Lives, 2004*, http://www.che-lives.com (September 12, 2005).

92   Ibid.

92   Anderson, p. 721

93   Anderson, *Che Guevara*, 624.

93   Guevara, *Self Portrait*, 266.

94   Anderson, *Che Guevara*, 736.

94   Ibid., 738.

94   Ariel Dorfman, "Che Guevara," *TIME's Heroes and Icons*, June 14, 1999, http://www.time.com/time/time100/heroes/ profile/guevara01.html (August 23, 2005).

96   Guevara, *Self Portrait*, 190.

96   Salas, *Fidel's Cuba*, 106.

98   Anderson, *Che Guevara*, 753.

100   Dorfman, "Che Guevara."

100–101   Ibid.

101   Ibid.

SELECTED BIBLIOGRAPHY

Anderson, Jon Lee. *Che Guevara: A Revolutionary Life*. New York: Grove Press, 1997.

Brenner, Philip, William M. LeoGrande, Donna Rich, and Daniel Siegel, eds. *The Cuba Reader: The Making of a Revolutionary Society*. New York: Grove Press, 1989.

"Che Guevara—Revolutionary." *British Broadcasting Company*. November 29, 2000. http://www.bbc.co.uk/dna/h2g2/A471241.

"Cuban Missile Crisis." *Thinkquest*. 1997. http://www.library.thinkquest.org/11046/days.html.

Dorfman, Ariel. "Che Guevara," *TIME's Heroes and Icons*. June 14, 1999. http://www.time.com/time/time100/heroes/profile/guevara01.html.

Granado, Alberto. *Traveling with Che Guevara: The Making of a Revolutionary*. New York: Newmarket Press, 2004.

Guevara, Ernesto Che. *The Motorcycle Diaries: Notes on a Latin American Journey*, Melbourne: Ocean Press, 2003.

———*Self Portrait: Che Guevara*. Edited by Victor Casaus. Melbourne: Ocean Press, 2004.

Llosa, Alvaro Vargas. "The Killing Machine," *New Republic*, July 9, 2005. http://www.independent.org/newsroom/article.asp?id=1535

Matthews, Herbert. "Cuban Rebel Is Visited in Hideout." *New York Times*, February 24, 1957.

Miranda, Carolina. "Che Lives!" *Time*, August 16, 2004. http://www.time.com/time/archive/preview/0,10987,994899,00.html?internatlid=related (August 23, 2005).

Reeves, Richard. "Thirteen Days in October." *New York Times*, October 8, 1997.

Salas, Osvaldo, and Roberto Salas. *Fidel's Cuba: A Revolution in Pictures*. New York: Thunder's Mouth Press; Hillsboro, OR: Beyond Words Publishing, 1998.

Suchlicki, Jaime. *Cuba: From Columbus to Castro and Beyond*. 5th ed. Washington, DC: Brassey's Inc., 2002.

Zinn, Howard. *A People's History of the United States: 1492–Present*. New York: Perennial Classics, 2003.

FURTHER READING
AND WEBSITES

Anderson, Catherine Corley. *John F. Kennedy*. Minneapolis: Twenty-First Century Books, 2004.

Butts, Ellen R., and Joyce R. Schwartz. *Fidel Castro*. Minneapolis: Twenty-First Century Books, 2005.

Campbell, Kumari. *Cuba in Pictures*. Minneapolis: Twenty-First Century Books, 2005.

Che Lives
http://www.che-lives.com
This site offers a brief biography of Che Guevara, some key speeches, and book excerpts.

The Cuban Missile Crisis: Fourteen Days in October.
http://www.library.thinkquest.org/11046/days.html
This website offers extensive details and background about the Cuban missile crisis.

Leonard, Thomas M. *Castro: The Cuban Revolution*. Westport, CT: Greenwood Press, 1999.

Sherman, Josepha. *The Cold War*. Minneapolis: Twenty-First Century Books, 2004.

Streissguth, Tom. *Argentina in Pictures*. Minneapolis: Twenty-First Century Books, 2003.

TIME 100: Heroes and Icons.
http://www.time.com/time/time100/heroes
This site lists and describes the one hundred people *TIME* magazine considers the most important of the twentieth century.

INDEX

OTHER TITLES FROM LERNER AND BIOGRAPHY®:

Ariel Sharon
Arnold Schwarzenegger
The Beatles
Benito Mussolini
Benjamin Franklin
Bill Gates
Billy Graham
Carl Sagan
Che Guevara
Chief Crazy Horse
Colin Powell
Daring Pirate Women
Edgar Allan Poe
Eleanor Roosevelt
Fidel Castro
Frank Gehry
George Lucas
George W. Bush
Gloria Estefan
Hillary Rodham Clinton
Jacques Cousteau
Jane Austen
Jesse Ventura
J. K. Rowling
Joseph Stalin
Latin Sensations

Legends of Dracula
Legends of Santa Claus
Malcolm X
Mao Zedong
Mark Twain
Maya Angelou
Mohandas Gandhi
Napoleon Bonaparte
Nelson Mandela
Osama bin Laden
Pope Benedict XVI
Queen Cleopatra
Queen Elizabeth I
Queen Latifah
Rosie O'Donnell
Saddam Hussein
Stephen Hawking
Thurgood Marshall
Tiger Woods
Tony Blair
Vladimir Putin
Wilma Rudolph
Winston Churchill
Women in Space
Women of the Wild West
Yasser Arafat

ABOUT THE AUTHOR

Kate Havelin is a writer, runner, and political activist who lives in St. Paul, Minnesota, with her husband and two sons. She is active in grassroots advocacy groups, including the Million Mom March, a group concerned with gun violence. She has run ten marathons and written fourteen books for young people, plus one running trails guidebook for adults.

PHOTO ACKNOWLEDGMENTS

The images in this book are used with permission of: © Keystone/Hulton Archive/Getty Images, pp. 2, 6, 56, 58, 88; Library of Congress, pp. 9 (LC-USZ62-72042), 27 (LC-USZ62-108432); © Hubert Stadler/CORBIS, p. 13; Laura Westlund, p. 14; © Kurt Hutton/Picture Post/Hulton Archive/ Getty Images, p. 15; © AP|Wide World Photos, pp. 18, 52, 63, 83, 90; © Evans/Three Lions/ Hulton Archive/Getty Images, p. 22; © Bettmann/CORBIS, pp. 25, 42, 73, 78, 93; © Robert Fried, p. 30; © Hulton Archive/Getty Images, pp. 34, 37; © Van der Heyden Collection/Independent Picture Service, p. 38; © Tim McGuire/CORBIS, p. 45; © Lee Lockwood/Time Life Pictures/Getty Images, p. 47; The Illustrated London News, p. 51; © CORBIS SYGMA, p. 54; © STF/AFP/Getty Images, p. 61; © George Silk/Time Life Pictures/Getty Images, p. 68; © AFP/Getty Images, pp. 86, 95; © John R. Kreul Collection/Independent Picture Service, pp. 96, 97; © Sam Lund/Independent Picture Service, pp. 98, 100.
Front cover: © Joseph Scherschel/ Time Life Pictures/Getty Images.
Back cover: © Central Press/Hulton Archive/Getty Images.

WEBSITES

Website addresses in this book were valid at the time of printing. However, because of the nature of the Internet, some addresses may have changed or sites may have closed since publication. While the author and Publisher regret any inconvenience this may cause readers, no responsibility for any such changes can be accepted by the author or Publisher.